In Search
of My
Parent

Tina P.

WESTBOW
PRESS®
A DIVISION OF THOMAS NELSON
& ZONDERVAN

WestBow Press books may be ordered through booksellers or by contacting:

WestBow Press
A Division of Thomas Nelson & Zondervan
1663 Liberty Drive
Bloomington, IN 47403
www.westbowpress.com
844-714-3454

[Scripture quotations are] from the New Revised Standard Version
Bible, copyright © 1989 the Division of Christian Education of
the National Council of the Churches of Christ in the United
States of America. Used by permission. All rights reserved.

ISBN: 978-1-6642-1265-7 (sc)
ISBN: 978-1-6642-1264-0 (hc)
ISBN: 978-1-6642-1266-4 (e)

Library of Congress Control Number: 2020922545

Print information available on the last page.

WestBow Press rev. date: 11/25/2020

Chapter 1

My name is Tina, a young girl growing up in a single parent home. The abandonment of growing up not knowing my father would make me miss out of on the joys of having my father walk me down the aisle on my wedding day. My father made me feel like I was not accepted and loved. In the end I would choose men who were just like my father.

As I sat on the floor with my hand over my head, and my head in my lap, and I watched Frank, my husband walked out the door. I can still recall the words he said. "You are no good, you are worthless, I found a woman better than you", and he was gone.

As I sat there feeling jilted and abandoned, my whole world falling apart, I decided that I must go searching for answers, I must seek help. "For it was you God, who formed my inward parts: you knit me together in my mother's womb. (psalm 139:13)

At birth I only weighted two and a half pounds I was so small, my mother could not hold me with her bare hands, so she had to ask the nurse for a pillow to lay me on, in order to lie next to me. After work my Dad stopped by the hospital to visit my Mom and his newborn daughter. When his wife handed him this tiny "thing", he took one look at his baby girl and said, "we are not flying in God's face, but it would have been better if she had died."

What would make a father wish his newborn baby dead? No matter how small this child was. Perhaps it was not the size of the baby that scared him, but maybe it was the four children he had at home including an eleven-month-old baby terrified him and being the sole bread winner. Whatever the case, Whatever the reasoning, if I know one thing, I know that I was unwanted by my father, from birth.

My mom said that after she left the hospital she never gave me her breast milk, but will go to the store and buy short green bananas, pronounced "maugh faugh Baugh", add potatoes and puree them with her breast milk and fed it to me.

I guess it worked, because before I was three months old, I was so big my mother, could not hold me by herself.

"Pastor, I grew up being obese all my life" I told Pastor Neverson. "People would laugh and call me demeaning names, even my own family. Many times, I cried, and it was in time like these that I really missed and needed my father. I felt so alone and lonely, but my daddy was never there to hold me and comfort me. He was always working, "making money" as he puts it, and was never there when I needed him the most. I never had a shoulder to cry on. He was never around", I sobbed.

Chapter 2

I was born in a small country called Sport Park Island. When my mother got pregnant again with her last child, my father encouraged her to go back to Carib Island.

Carib Island got its name from the Caribs, the first inhabitants who lived on that Island. This was my mom's native homeland. My mom moved there with her four children, so she could get the help she needed from her mother and sister. Her husband told her he will stay on a little longer to work and promised to join her later.

On the day of the trip back to her Homeland, I remembered my mom dressing us, and told us that we were going for a ride in a big boat. I got all excited and said, "Mom, where are we going"? I kept asking her over and over. I never stopped until my Mom answered because I always wanted answers. My mother told me, "we are going to see my grandmother, who lived in another country". I got all excited again as I always wanted to meet my grandmother as she was my only grandparent alive. "Yes! I am going to see mama", and I started jumping up and down in my little childish ways. When we got to the to the place where the boat was disembarking, there were plenty of boats in the sea, some noticeably big, some not so big, and some small. As far as my eyes could see, there was just blue water. Mom had a lot of suitcases and baggage, so Dad helped her put the suitcases and luggage on the boat, then kissed us and told us to be good for Mommy. Mom with her four children, Winston, Irwin. Lou-Lou and me boarded the boat. She was five months pregnant again, and had already sent home Cay, her first child, to mama when Winston and Irwin were born.

As we got on, the boat was rocking side by side, so I felt sick in my stomach. I told mom "my tummy is hurting". Mom opened her bag and give me a biscuit and told that would make my tummy feel better. The big boat started moving and with the movement of the boat, I fell asleep. When I woke up mom fed us and then took us outside to another part of the boat, where a lot people were seated. I started playing and making friends with the other children. This kept my mind off the rocking of the boat, because we now had friends to play with, while mom was engaged talking with the adults. It seemed like we were on the boat forever. We slept, woke up, slept again. I kept wondering when would we get to this other country and kept asking my mom, "are we there yet"? Then I heard a male voice announced, Look out the window we spotted Carib Island; I look out the window and all I saw was a big rock, I was thinking where are we going to live? Are we going to live on this big rock? It took several more hours before the male voice announced "Welcome to Carib Island."

We all got off the boat, and mom paid a man who had a cart made from wood to get her suitcases and baggage to take them to a car. I asked, "where are we going? how far is mama house", my mother told me that mama lived in the rural area, which they called "country". She said it was about forty minutes away and we would get there soon.

When we arrived in the village where my grandmother lives, the car left us on the side of the main road. We had to walk down a narrow dirt road to get to mama's house. The villagers came out to see us, including our cousin who was slightly autistic, and mentally challenged. She ran down to the house and exclaimed "mama, they come, some red, some black, some brown, them all color mama".

My grandmother was a short woman with gray hair, and she look so old to me. There was also another woman, who introduced herself as auntie Tess, my mother's sister.

Pastor Neverson glanced at her clock, and then I realized that my session was almost to an end.

"Tina how are you feeling now?" Pastor Neverson asked.

I became quiet for a few minutes and then I answered, "much better, much better." Pastor smiled and said,

"O. K see you the same time next week?"

I answered "yes."

Chapter 3

"I realized I had another sister by the name of Cay. My father was Thomas Richman, who was born in 1905 in a small town called Lilliput in Carib Island. My Mother Adella was born in a small agricultural village of sunny vile in Carib Island. My parents migrated to Sport park Island, where they met and fell in love, married, and give birth to their first child Cay Alica Younda. When Cay was two years old, my mother had her second child named Winston. One year later my parents had their third child, Irwin."

"With three small children, my mother had her hands full, so my parents decided to send their oldest child, Cay, home to Carib Island to live with my grandmother. The problem is my parents never told us about Cay, until that day when I was introduced to her at my grandmother's house. Cay looked shy at first, but then she came over, hugged us, and started talking to us. She was a very protecting and caring sister, but she never forgave our mom for sending her away."

Chapter 4

Because of the memory I had of Sport Park Island, it was so easy to fall in love with Carib Island. My family lived in an extended family household with my grandmother, my aunt and her husband. Two months after arriving in Carib Island, my mother gave birth to her last child Linda."

"I remembered while growing up, there were only Auntie Tess as we called her, her real name was Theresa, and my grandmother (mama) but my mother was not there. Whenever I cried and asked for my mother, my grandmother explained what happened to my mother. During that time when you have a baby you were supposed to stay in bed for nine days after the baby was born. The midwife would band the mother' belly with a piece of white cloth for three months which was a tradition. My grandmother explained that after the nine days, mom went to town (the City) transportation were very scarce in those days, so she had to walk about two miles to the bus stop. It was storming that day and my mom got caught up in the storm. Just having a nine-days old baby she caught a cold and got sick. in those days people in the Islands were dying from the common cold. There was insufficient medical care, doctors were scarce, and you are only able to see the doctor in real emergencies. My mom had to go to a facility until she was better. My grandmother depended and believed in her homemade medicine when we were sick. What I like most about living in my grandmother's house hold was on rainy days when we could not go outside to play, so Mama would put us on her lap, some of us would sit on the floor in a ring circle and mama would tell us " old-time" stories."

Chapter 5

"Our small village in Green park Valley, is incredibly beautiful. In the morning you can see the sunrise, and in the evening, you see the pretty colors of the sun dancing in the sky as the sun sets. You could see acres of lands cultivated with agricultural crops such as green vegetables, bananas, potatoes, dasheen and eddoes. In the afternoon, I love to listen to the music of the birds as they sing on their way home at evening time. What I used to admire most as a child is the way the birds stayed together in a cluster."

"I always felt safe growing up in Green Park Valley where the community looked out for each other. It was difficult to misbehave in the presence of an adult as the adult had the right to spank that child and send him/her home to the parents. That child dared not complained to the parents that "Miss So and So "beat (spank) him/her as the parents would inquire about the reason why this happened, and the child would be getting another spanking. In those days, spanking was a positive form of discipline. The motto was "It takes two persons to have a child, but a village to raise it."

Chapter 6

My daddy was not there, only my mom, and their six children. When I asked mom "where is my daddy and when is he coming", my mom told me Dad was staying a little while longer, to make enough money to take care of us. Family is especially important to me, and my family protected us at all cost and were always there for us. "Pastor Neverson, I love my family"; Pastor Neverson nodded her head and said, "I am sure you love your family Tina."

"Pastor Neverson, life was not all bad, there were good and bad days, when life was good, I felt blessed and close to God. My mom made us know the Lord at a young age. She sent us to church and Sunday school. As soon as I started to face trouble and tribulation and going through trials, I would detach myself from God and want to handle it on my own. To me a God I could not see was not real. He was not around to be there for me and give me the power and strength to face my struggles and see me through, that is what I thought! God was just like my dad who was not there for me." Pastor Neverson scratched her head and asked "Tina, do you think that God abandon you too". I answered "although I knew that God is the closest person to a father, but I had little faith in Him and still could not trust Him wholeheartedly" Tina continued her story.

"One day at Kindergarten, the teacher came in and said children its story time. I loved story time it was my favorite time in school. The teacher continued to introduce the story. Our story today is about a little girl name Cinderella. I listened with anticipation, and after she finished telling the story, I started to cry. When the teacher asked me what was the matter, and why was I crying; in a teary voice I sobbed, where's her daddy"?

Pastor Neverson seeing the hurt in my eyes and seeing how emotional I got, she asked me, "did you tell your mother about the story". "No, in those days, children were mostly seen and not heard so I kept it to myself".

"Many times, I would notice my mother crying;

seeing my mother cried was very painful for me. Pastor Neverson, my daddy never came. It was painful to see my mother crying but could not ask her if she was all right, because in those days it was not in a child's place to question an adult, much less her parent. All I wanted to do, was to go and hug my mother and cry with her and tell her it will be alright, even if I never believed it myself. Pastor, it was so hard to see my mother crying. All I could do was walk away. So, with that I could not trust my father and really could not trust anyone, especially men, I swore that I will never love a man and will never get married."

"I was so discouraged, in time of despair and loneliness, I missed the security of knowing a father's love and care for me when I was hurting. I missed a father who will listen to my needs, hugged me and told me it will be alright. He was not there then, and now he is still not there."

Pastor Neverson interrupted, "so how did you all survive financially, if your dad never came home and your mother was sick who took care of the bills"?

"MY dad never came home, but made arrangement for the company, he was working for, to send his pension check to my mother to take care of us. After mom came out of the hospital the money she received from my dad's pension, was able to support us in an upper-class lifestyle. My mom bought a property in Decasa hill, as we called it with two and a half acres of land and a large three-bedroom board house".

"Mom moved out of mama's house and moved into her own home in Decasia hill. It was like living on a farm, my mom had farmers cultivate the lands for her and planted small crops, like, tomatoes, cabbage, lettuce, peppers and chive. They also planted, potatoes, yam, eddoes and dasheen. There were also breadfruit and coconut, and mango trees on the lands. She never sold the produce from the lands but kept them for her own use. She bought cattle, goats and pigs and give them to the men in the village to raise for half. She also raised her own chicken in the back yard, for meat and eggs; she raises everything for her own use. She did not have to buy meat, vegetable and eggs, because all came from her back yard. When she reaped the produce of the land, she would call the neighbors and share. We had everything we wanted; we were financially secure, because my dad check kept coming, we lived an upper-class life, had maids waiting on our every need. Every day we ate together as a family, around the dining table and had to recite the Grace before and after meals, but I always noticed the empty chair, which represented my father's place around the table. Thankfully, it was easier dealing with the rejection of my father, because I had my mom, but it was the absence of my father that affected me most. I had everything I wanted, we were rich, yet I felt poor. My friends who were so much poorer I, felt that they were so much richer, because they had their two parents living in their homes and I only had one, I was so jealous of my friends for that reason.

Chapter 7

Finally, my dad came home to visit, and he did not even stay up Decasa hill with us. He stayed by his family in the city but would come to visit us. I never remembered that he ever took us to visit with his family where he was staying. But I remembered he paid me a twenty –fine cent (a quarter) to stop sucking my finger and he spanked me, when my sister and I were fighting; we were fighting over some silly thing and dad was cheering us on, but when he told us to stop and we did not, because no one wanted to take the last lash. He got up took off his belt and spanked both of us. Although it hurt, it felt good that dad was home and was taking on the father's role to discipline us. As I said before, growing up in the Island spanking was a positive rule for discipline.

He was now living in Crown Island, which we did not know, because he never wrote to us. When he was leaving to go back to Crown Island, my oldest sister took the younger ones, to the wharf in City to see my dad leave. With tears in my eyes, I watched my father board a big white ship. I never saw my father again. Then I realized despite everything I loved my father'

'Pastor Neverson, one day I remembered playing in the garden and was trying to climb a breadfruit tree, when my brother Winston came and put me up in the tree."

"Wow!" Pastor Neverson exclaimed "how did you feel being up in the tree".

"I felt like being on top of the world looking down at creation. That was a really nice feeling."

Pastor Neverson laughed.

"Pastor wait until you hear the rest of the story. My brother was standing below the tree with outstretched arms telling me to jump. I love my brother and trusted him. He acted not only as a big brother, but as a father figure to us, protected us at all cost. I knew my brother will never hurt me, but I was wrong, I jumped knowing my brother would catch me. He did not. He pulled away his hands and let me fall."

"what!" Pastor Neverson exclaimed, "so what did you do?"

I started to cry, "I am going to tell mommy."

This was when he picked me up and carried me to the faucet we had outdoors and washed off my wounds. Then he carried me inside to the medicine chest and dressed my wounds. Pastor guessed what my brother told me after he dressed my wounds. He said he was sorry, nope! He told me, never trust a man, not even your own brother."

Chapter 8

"I got sick and started having tummy pain, so my sister Cay took me to the doctor because mom never left the house, maybe because she was sick. The doctor admitted me to the hospital; Cay used to go to a High School in the city and she would come and visit me every evening. Nurse Sam, a friend of my mother, was working in that hospital and she would also visit with me every day and bring me ice cream. Another person who visited me and was a young woman dressed in white carrying a bible. She told me God loves me so much, that he sends his son Jesus to die for me." "Although I used to go to Church and Sunday school and learn about God and Jesus, it was the first time I believe that I was a child of God and that he loves me so much that, He sent his son to die to save me. I prayed the sinner's prayer with that young woman, and I left that hospital filled with the Holy Spirit. Pastor Neverson that young woman changed my life completely."

Pastor Neverson said "Praise the Lord"

"For every purpose there is a season and a time for everything under the sun a time to die". I remembered reading this in the bible."

Yes", Pastor Neverson replied you are so right Ecclesiastes 3: 1-2

"There is a time for every season, and life has its season, and I know that everything that has life must die. When I was, growing up I used to hear these saying; "time waits on no man", "time and season will pass away", I would add to it, and so do men, by this statement Pastor Neverson laugh. Someone once said. "What is new today would be old and absolute and gone tomorrow" and I remembered singing this song in school "All thing which live below the sky music along shall live."

This was the saddest day of my life on 31 October 1961 with no sign of illness, my mom left without even saying goodbye and went to glory to be with the Lord. I remembered it as if it were yesterday. I was sitting around the dining table doing my homework my other siblings had gone to church for rehearsal for the harvest festival was on the following Sunday. Nurse Sam, a very good friend of my mother, was with her, only because Mom had requested her to come to see her on that day. I had a lot of homework to do for school and did not want to go to rehearsal. My mom tried to convince me to go to rehearsal, but to no avail. I wanted to stay at home to do my homework. I loved school and always wanted to succeed."

It was about seven thirty, mom and nurse Sam were in the living room talking, when mom called to me ; "Tina could you go and bring my dinner for me please", I did not wanted to get up so I sucked my teeth. My mom heard and told me not to bother she will get it for herself. Worst of all mom did not argue with me or call me rude or even corrected me for sucking my teeth to her. She got up and came into the kitchen for her dinner. This made me feel badly. She and Nurse Sam joined me around the dini*ng room table*. Mom liked Dixie biscuit and there was always a can of Dixie biscuit on the table. Nurse Sam opens the can of biscuit and took out some of the biscuit, my mom, and I asked her for two of the biscuit, and Nurse Sam handed us only two biscuit. When we start complaining why she only gave us two biscuit, she jokingly said it was what we ask for.

Mom cleared her throat and went in her bedroom, then she called out "Sam come I am dying" I am dying was a slang for mom, anything that happened to her, she was dying.

Nurse Sam said, "When your mother is dying, she won't have mouth to talk" and with that she laughed and went to mom's assistance.

As soon as Nurse Sam got into the room, I heard her calling mom by her name as if she were waking her from a deep sleep. I stopped doing my homework, put down the pen, and started listening; Now all kind of thoughts started coming to my mind, "mom cannot fall asleep so quickly I wander if she is dead, no mom cannot die so easily". I kept on wrestling with my thoughts. My mom cannot leave us now, dad already left, but if mom died daddy will come home. I quickly dismissed that thought out of my mind, because I did not want to think that my mother was dead.

When Nurse Sam came out of the room she said, "Tina it looks like your mommy is dead". I started screaming, "No nurse Sam no! mom can't die so easily" Nurse Sam held on to me and carried me into the bedroom. Mom was lying on the floor lifeless. She was dead. I screamed so hard that it brought out the whole neighborhood. In a minute, the house was filled with people. Some of the neighbors helped Nurse Sam put mom on the bed. The question that was always in my mind did my mother knew she was going to die that day, so she asked nurse Sam to come to be with her, or was it just a coincident? I will never know. After many years thinking and missing mom, I wrote this poem.

"You never said you were leaving
You left without a warning
You never said goodbye.

You were gone before I knew it.
Only God knows why?
A million times, I called your name
So many times, I cried, and asked why"
This poem bought back memories of my mom, after all these years,
so I added this other verse to this poem

"I light a candle every year
In memory of you.
For the many things, you taught me,
And the many things you do.
For part of me went with you,
The day God called you home."

Chapter 9

"After the funeral, family and neighbors stayed on at the house for forty days, as it was a custom. After the forty days, the family got together, the big discussion had to be made, who will take each child, like if they were auctioning the children the adults saying which child they wanted. Pastor, this made me incredibly sad, losing my mom was hard, but now losing my sibling was worst. I ran in my bedroom and started crying all over again. Pastor Neverson shook her head. Then Auntie Tess spoke up and said who take one must take all. I am not separating my sister 'children". They all exclaimed "six children Tess!"

She said, "I will take them", so we all went to live with Auntie Tess except Linda who was already staying with Auntie Clair.

"When mom was alive, we were living an upper-class life. We ate the best, eating with knife and fork, practicing table manners was our lifestyle. We wore the best and we had housemaids waiting on us night and day. Pastor Neverson, life was good we were living like big shots."

Pastor Neverson laughed.

"This was when things changed drastically".

Pastor Neverson became serious again.

Living with my aunt and my grandmother life changed so drastically my aunt was the poorest of all the family and she had just taken on the task of caring for five children with no mother and father. The day of mom funeral Cay cried and beat her chest, and said "no mother, no father what will become of six children" I missed mom so much, but my only hope and consolation, now mom is dead, daddy will come home to make sure we are a alright, but dad never came. But would write to us every month and send me money I would open the letters, took out the money that my father sent and throw the letters in an empty old wooden suit case I had, without reading the letters. I saved those unread letters for years. One day I was alone at home, my aunt went to the garden, and my sister went to school, I felt alone, rejected, and discouraged. I took my old shabby bible and began to read psalm 27 in the King James Version. "When my father and mother forsake me then the Lord will take me up". I took the old, wooded suitcase, from its hiding place, carried it outside in the garden, pure kerosene oil on it, and lit it on fire. I screamed as I watch the fire blazed, then as the fire subsided, all that left was ashes. I dug a hole and throw the ashes in the hole and said, "dust to dust, ashes to ashes" then I covered the hole with the ashes, to me it was like my father was dead."

Chapter 10

" I love and enjoyed school until Auntie Tess came up with the idea that I could not learn and it was a waste of time sending me to school, because I was dumb, so I had to stay at home doing all the house work while my other sister went to school, and my aunt went in the garden to work.

After I finished the house work I would run away, and go to school risking getting six lashes with a leather strap for late coming. Then one day I spoke to my class teacher, He, was dating my older sister Cay at the time, so he worked out a plan for me. The plan was when I was not at school, he will send my home-work and the work I missed to me to make up and do it at home, it was like home schooling.

JRod one of my class mate volunteered to bring

my school work for me and took them back to school the next day to be graded, if they did any new lesson, especially math, he will say to me "Are you comimg down the spring for water", J Rod was living close to the spring.

Even if the bucket was full with water I will throw it away, when no body was watching, I would call out to Auntie Tess and told her I was going down the spring for water. When I got to the spring J Rod was there waiting for me, and he will teach me the lesson I missed, with that I never failed a class. I remembered I got the worst spanking when someone told my aunt that I used to run away and go to school; up to this day I do not know who told her, so this was the end of of my home schooling. I grew up with a low self- esteem believing I was dumb, and diden't have a brain."

I pulled out this old faded photograph from my old shabby bag and handed it to Pastor Neverson, I spoke with pride, about my old school, I said to pastor Neverson, I remembere my old principal used to tell us that, " school days and courtship days are the two best tim in life", Then I turned to pastor Neverson and said " I missed out on my school days. Would I ever be able to get that back".

"This was my favourite poem about my school. I can still remember the words. Do you want to hear it Pastor Neverson"?"

"Yes Tina I would love to hear it"?

"O.K". my face lit up as I became excited "O.K I will say it for you".

"I'll honor yet the school I knew

> The land of youth and dreams
> To greet again the rule I knew,
> Before I took the streets.
> Though long I missed the sight of her,
> My heart will not forget,
> I'll lost the old delight of her.
> I'll keep her honor yet"
> (From grade 6 Western Royal Reader).

"Isn'that a nice poem Pastor Neverson. I loved that poem".

"Yes Tina that is a very nice poem."

Pastor Neverson turned to me and said, "Tina this is enough for today. I will see you back here on Wednesday morning at 10. A.m. Do you think you can do that."

I answered "Yes pastor Neverson".

Pastor Neverson said to me, " In the next few days I want you to read psalm 139. could you do that"?

"Yes pastor I replied" .

Pastor Neverson closed with a prayer and I was dismissed from the session.

Chapter 11

On Wednesday I was ready for my next session, I was so excited to meet with Pastor Neverson, because I never told anyone what I was going through. I was able to talk about my life for the first time. Pastor Neverson was waiting for me, when I entered the church on Wednesday. "Good morning Pastor" I greated her.

"Good Morning Tina, how are you today".

"Pastor, I am wonderful" ! "you know what the Psalm say that you give me to read".

'What does it say Tina"? Pastor Neverson replied . "That God Knew me when I was in my mother's belly and God saw all that I was going through"."

"Yes He did",

After a prayer Tina continued telling her story .

"On Saturdays I had to go in the river to wash the

dirty laundry, while my sisters went for typing lessons in Green Park valley." I would soak the clothes on a big stone and take piece by piece and wash them with my hands. After I finishing washing the whitw clothes I would soap them a second time and put them on a big stone or the flat grass in the sun to bleach; there were nothing like clorax or bleach in those days. When I get home from the river, if the clothes were not white or clean enough when auntie Tess examine them, I would get a beating with piece of the wet clothes, and auntie Tess would throw the clothes on the ground and stamp on them until they are black with dirt and then send me back in the river to wash them a second time. So Pastor, I always made sure that the clothes were all white and clean before I leave the river.

Pastor Neverson nodded her head "sure"

"In those days housework was particularly challenging and quite difficult. We did not have any stove or coal pot to cook on, so I would had to go to the mountain to collect wood for the fire so I would have to fan the fire with two pieces of breadfruit leaves or stoop down and blow on the firewood; so it can blaze

"Pastor Neverson you know what"?

"What Tina" she replied

"Although Life was hard, it was not hard all the time. I had some good times, but I had to work hard for it.

"Tell me about the good times "Pastor Neverson exclaimed.

"O. K". Tina spoke with excitement. "On holidays we would take bus trips (bus excursion) to the beaches, I love going to the beach and to La Soufriere, an active volcano on the island. But I was only allowed to go if I completed all my chores. On the day before the trip, I will make sure all the chores were done and everything was spick and span. We would pack picnic basket with rice and fried chicken, ginger and sorrel beer, cakes, and do not forget the strong rum. This strong rum was 100 proof alcohol. This was a time for sharing; everybody would share their food and drinks, especially the strong rum. The bus would depart about 8 a.m. to take us to the picnic site. We would start drinking liquor, rum, beer, and Guinness whatever was on the bus and continue drinking until we reach the picnic site. By the time we got to the picnic site almost everybody was drunk. We spend half of the day picnicking and in the afternoon we would we change in our best party clothes, and then the bus would take us to the bar in the neighboring town, where we will party all night and get back home by midnight or later. This was my way of rebelling. I got an inch, and I took a mile. Drinking the alcohol made me feel good and most of all taking my mind off all that I was going through at home. I did not care anymore where my daddy was. I realized that my daddy did not love me and was never coming to get me. I had a low self-esteem, so I drank alcohol to help me to socialize and to be appreciated by others. That's what I thought. That was the biggest mistake I made, Then I realized that alcohol was not the answer; Jesus was, and from that, moment I made a pledge never to drink alcohol again. This was the kind of bus that took us on the trip; in fact, this kind of bus was the only means of transportation in my time.

"Something else I did for fun was, after Sunday School which was a must, my friends and sibling and I will go for long walks. Our favorite venue was to walk through Aerie. Aerie was a small, long narrow strip of land which separated two neighboring villages. Being on the hilltop and looking down at the beauty of green vegetation in the valley below reminded me of the splendor of God's creation. I took for granted God amazing work in my life. Just as He cares for the flowers and the trees, He cares for me too. So, I reflected on God as my father, and pastor Neverson that's what Psalm 139 is saying that God formed me and knew me even before I was born, and I am fearfully and wonderfully made. Isn't that wonderful Pastor Neverson?"

"Yes, Tina that is so wonderful".

Then I sat down and write this poem. I love to put my thoughts in writing poems

God's Beauty by Tina

"As we walked together my friends and I along a dirt and deserted road

With no one insight

There was only room enough for two

Along the winding street

We kept going forward, to see where it would lead

The narrow path before us Cover with carpet of grass and weed

No feet had passed that way

No sign of civilization

Yet the beauty of the villages below

Reminds me of the beauty of God's creations

My heart was filled with wander

As my feet, softly touch on carpet of moss.

When I was halfway across

I looked back to see how far God has brought me

Along life rugged way

A bright flash of color caught my eyes

As I reach on the other side

Horns of cars driving back and forth

Tina P.

Laughter of children as they play. Lights everywhere
Yet I will never forget how beauty abound
Along that deserted road
My friends and I have found."

Chapter 12

"Splendor abound in the valley on moonlight nights, all the children would come out and play "Coopie" and ring games in our back yard. Those were the days when there were no radios and TV, and children would have to go outside and play. they played games like:

Amy Amy coming down

I lost my gloves on a Saturday night,

Jane and Louisa will soon come home, and many more. The parents would cook breadnut and roasted corn for the children while we played. All the other children's parents would come out and enjoy the games and watched the children play, but I would notice my missing father.

Christmas was a very festive season, but, as for me

it has lost its value, everyone is caught up in the hassle and bustle of decorating the houses and what to eat and drink and lost the real meaning of Christmas. It is Jesus birthday, and Jesus should be the center of this festive season.

From December 1, I had to strip the window curtain and leave the windows bare. I will have to wash every window in the house, scrape and varnish every chair, and then I will have to scrub the walls and the floors. I would take a hoe and scrape the moss off the dirt yard. I made broom with coconut pointer to sweep the yard.

Christmas was a very festive season, with lot of food to eat and a lot of ginger beer, sorrel beer and mauby. We had to collect our own bottles. We will be looking all day in the garden and underneath the houses for empty Juicy bottles. We had to collect twenty-four bottles to get a box of Juicy and each child will have the full box "Juicy" for himself. You also had to get the big bottles and wash them, to put the ginger beer, mauby and sorrel beer. As previously mentioned, each child will have to wash their own bottles, and again each child will get a bottle of mauby, a bottle of ginger beer and a bottle of sorrel beer. This was a real treat. I loved Christmas because I loved to eat. it was the only time I had enough to eat and drink. Auntie Tess would go to town and sell the produce she got from the lands to buy fabric to make new curtain for the windows. She will buy new linoleum for the floor and paint to paint the walls. The night before Christmas Eve, the butchers will kill the cow and the pig at about midnight and sell the meat. My uncle Auntie Tess's husband was a butcher, and I liked to stay up late, to see them kill the cow and pig, I remembered, one year as they were killing the bull and stabbed it in the throat with the knife, the bull got away, and started chasing us. We had to run for our lives. I never knew I could run fast. The bull ran for about a few hundred yards until it dropped dead. In the morning my aunt will take me to the river to clean the cattle and pig intestines, and when she get home from the river, she will boil water to clean the cattle skin to make soup on Boxing day. My aunt will also take the largest tripe from the cow and mixed farine and the blood from the cow and seasoned it with salt and pepper and grind seasoning and make blood pudding; I loved blood pudding. It is like sausage, and you could fry it over and eat with bread for breakfast.

The people in the village would start lining up from midnight to buy their meat, and when they got home, they would kill the biggest fowl in the yard that they were rearing for months for Christmas dinner.

After baking, I had to scrub the pots and pans with coconut fiber and ashes until you can see your face through them, then I would have to go the spring for water, to full the two water drums that were in the yard, Then I have to sweep the yard; everything had to be spic and span.

About a month before Christmas, the Serenades went door to door caroling for money. They would sing carols and say speeches like

"Christmas is coming the geese are getting fat

Please put a penny in the old man hat.

If not a penny, a half penny would do.

If not a half penny, may God still bless you"?

Nine mornings before Christmas, people from the village and neighboring villages would come out about four a.m., and play steel pan, and shack- shack and other musical instruments in the street, and the villagers will come out dancing in the street.

The worst part in all this is that everything is left to be done on Christmas eve; The first thing Auntie Tess will do when she get up on Christmas eve, after cleaning the animals tripe, she will start baking, I had to help with the washing of the butter, When I finished mixing the ingredient for the cake, I will knead the flour to make the bread and then put them in a drum oven to bake; again each child will get a big bread and a big pan of cake. We used this oven back then. This was a learning experience for me, because today I am a good cook, and I can bake." Again, I pulled out the pictures I had in my shabby bag that I saved all these years.

It was a lot of hard work, but with all those goodies, it was extremely rewarding. In the night when the baking and everything is finish outside, we will go into the house to start decorating the house. I had to shine the glass windows with white vinegar and newspaper, when I finish you could see your face through the glass. Some people had wooden windows, but we had glass windows. Then the new linoleum covered with paper will placed over the old wooden floor the children will jumped on the linoleum to ripped off the paper this was fun. About fore day morning (just before dawn) the serenades would come, and you will open up your home and they would come in and have a treat, with the bread and cake and the roasted pork and the blood pudding, then the rum. At Christmas everyone shared. When they left, we had to do a fresh set of cleaning all over again, because everything had to be spic and span for Christmas morning.

We dressed in our pretty dress we got for Christmas, and go to 5 a.m. Sunrise service, if we are lucky, we would see the sun dance. There was a myth that the cow used to kneel, some people claimed that they saw it, but to me it was just a myth. When I got back home from church, I was so tired, from not sleeping the night before, all I wanted to do was to go back to bed. Christmas day was the only day I could rest. Auntie Tess would do the cooking. In the evening after dinner we will go visiting house to house. This was a custom, and if no one came to your house, you felt embarrassed and left out. On boxing day, our parent would send us to valley community hall for fete, but with a curfew, we had to be back home by six P.M. Again, I made sure all my chaos was done. The last dance was at six o clock and my friends and I, always waited for the last dance and then ran all the way home."

Pastor Neverson laughed

"Pastor Neverson! I remembered one boxing day as we were running home it was raining and we were already late getting home, so we took a short cut home. We had to cross a river to get over on the other side, when we got to the river, "river come down "as they used to say in the island and we could not cross, so we had to run all the way back from and started our journey all over again, so that made us really late.

Pastor Neverson smiled "so what happened when you got home"?

"Pastor Neverson we got the finest spanking and were band from going to fete".

Pastor Neverson said "Tina can I ask you a question" "sure Pastor Neverson, anything"! I replied

She asked "what is river come down"

I started laughing; "It's when it it's raining and storming and the water in the shallow stream raises and overflow on the banks of the river. Pastor Neverson, that is extremely dangerous, when river come down, it takes everything and everyone in its path including trees, houses or even people and wash them away".

Pastor Neverson nodded her head.

"Pastor! Do you want to hear another funny, but true story about running home from fete?"

"Yes Tina, I certainly do" answer Pastor Neverson.

"O.K listen to this one" Tina replied.

"One night after fete, we always stay over the time and then ran about five miles home. After fete, this boy had the brightest idea to accompany me half-way home. I told him no but to no avail because I did not even like him and I was already late getting home. I told him to turn back but he never did. When we got a few blocks from my aunt's house, this was when this dude decided to turn back. I was so mad and worst of all I could not tell him I will get in trouble.

"Why"? Pastor Neverson exclaimed.

"Too much pride" I answered.

Pastor Neverson laughed.

When I got to my aunt Clair's house hoping my sister would be there waiting for me, but she did not. She went home without me, and so I was in real trouble now. Then I heard a bike. it was my brother's, so I waited for my him. He parked the bike and we walked into the house together. Pastor Neverson, my aunt did not ask me anything".

Pastor Neverson said "she thought you were with your brother"

"yep" and I started to laugh.

Chapter 13

Market day was a special day in Carib Island. People in Green park valley were mainly farmers and live by the land. They will grow their crops and take it to the market to sell. Many people will stay outside of the market and put their produce on the side of the street to sell, many people prefer to sell outside, because they claim that, they got better sale. When they sell all their produce or "load "as they call it, they will take the money and buy groceries to last for the week or until next market day.

They will try to make a dollar out of fifty cent, by looking for a bargain, at that time codfish or salt fish as we called it, Black fish and corn fish and sprat were cheap, so they will buy enough to last the week. They did not have to buy ground provision because they grew them and when breadfruit season is in these fish will go well with the roasted breadfruit. My favorite dish was roasted breadfruit and salt fish (codfish) make Bul-Jou. How to make bul-jou? Pastor Neverson asked

"That's a good question. You boil the salt fish and then soak it in some cold water to get out the salt, but not all of the salt, then you stew it down in oil, onion cut finely and then you season it with a little hot pepper s then you cut up a tomato and cucumber on the salt fish. We grew the tomatoes and cucumbers in our own back yard or in the mountain. What was also nice was the roasted breadfruit and roasted pork; not roasted in the oven, but on firewood; or roasted sprat. We used to throw the strong rum on the sprat to roast it. Pastor Neverson you know what sprat is, no Tina, what is sprat? Sprat is a small fish with many scales, and when you roast them with the strong run and season them with lime juice, salt, and pepper, it is the bum, you will also get a treat when Tri-Tri is in; Tri –Tri and roasted breadfruit is the bum! This could be used for any meal. Tea (breakfast), lunch, and dinner. Tina you are always saying it is the bum, what that mean? pastor Neverson askes, I started to laugh; That is a slang word which mean it is good.

The main food for breakfast, was penny bread and bush tea, if you are lucky on Sundays you might get coco tea, otherwise it was bush tea with roasted breadfruit or penny bread.

the farmers who rear goats and pigs like my uncle, usually rear them to kill. They will kill the pig and put a lot of salt and pepper on the meat and make corned pork and then sell it by the half a pound and pound then you can have roasted breadfruit and roast pork for dinner yummmmmmm, Pastor they take the pig feet, and the ears and make souse, the head and the tripe and made soup with it nothing is being thrown away. Sunday dinner was the best no matter how poor you were. Almost everyone ate the best meals on Sundays. On Saturday you will pick the pigeon Peas from the garden, you will get the young dasheen heart, which we called Callaloo to make barge. The menu for a typical Sunday meal in my house was rice and Peas, Callaloo barge, breadfruit or Irish potato salad and sweet potato and plantain on the side. For meat, either it could be chicken or whole fowl; pork, beef stew, or fish fried and stew over. As a child, I would look forward to Sunday dinner, which I had to cook."

"Growing banana was the main crop and almost ever farmer grew bananas this was what brought most families out of the poverty level. Banana day was a special day. You will cut the stem, take them out to the bus stop, and wait for the bus to take us to the banana station where you would sell the bananas. On banana day, many students would be automatically excused from school.

Chapter 14

P astor Neverson listened to Tina, with anticipation. Then said to me, "you said you grew up in a Christian home and you had to go to church, so how was your faith in all this, Tina" Pastor Neverson said to me

This is what I told her." I Knew the Lord as my heavenly father and felt that God was calling me to seek Him, I knew Him more as a father than my own father, but my question was how can I relate to God as a father, when my own father rejected, despised, and gave up his responsibilities as a father. How could I trust God as my father? The good news however, that my understanding of fatherhood is not limited to my earthly father, because he is not what defines a father. It is God.

"Praise the Lord Tina", Pastor Neverson replied.

I continued "I heard God call through a young woman whose name was Miss Dick, a young evangelist for Jesus Christ I was sick in the hospital and this young woman visited me every day and told me about the love of God and Jesus Christ HIS son. She told me that God is my father and that He loves me so much, He sent His only Son Jesus Christ to die for me. Although I was going to Church at an early age and wanted to trust God and have a relationship with Him, the abandonment I felt from my father prevented me from trusting God whole-heartedly. This was the first time I had a personal encounter with God and saw Him as my heavenly father and took Him as the earthly father I never had. I accepted Jesus Christ, God's Son as my personal Savior; I would talk to Him; I told Him everything that was bothering me. God and Jesus became my confidantes. When I could not talk to anyone else, I knew I could talk to God and I felt safe with Him. I saw Christ in that young woman and wanted to be just like her. This woman changed my life completely. I left the hospital filled with the Holy Spirit and began witnessing and handing out religious materials to my teachers and classmates."

Pastor Neverson said "Praise God"

Chapter 15

T he abandonment of my own father left a void in my heart. I was longing to love and to be loved. Therefore, I started reading Solomon love letters in the bible

My love life.

Set me a seal upon your heart

as a seal upon your arm

For love is stronger than death,

Passion fierce as the grave

Love flashes are flashes of fire,

Raging flames

Many waters cannot quench love

Neither can flood drown it.

If one offered for love all the wealth of his house

It will be utterly scorned"

Song of Solomon 8:6-7

"I had my first boyfriend at the age of fourteen, boys were the last thing on my mind, I felt ugly, and had no self-esteem. No one will ever love me. I was the ugly duckling, I would say. I did not go looking for love, but love found me.

It was a Saturday afternoon, Auntie Tess sent me up Decasa hill to the house where we used to live. My brothers were now living there, so she sent me to collect the dirty dishes up there, and to get some vegetables from the garden like cucumbers, tomatoes, sweet peppers carrots and chive and some young dasheen heart to make bargie for our Sunday dinner. "Decasa" was the name my brothers called our old home, and it was where all my brothers' friends used to hang out, especially on week-ends.

You can hear music miles from Decasa, but on this Saturday, there was no music, and everything were silent. This surprised me, but I figured no one was home. When I entered the house, no one was in sight, so I went into the room, which used to be the girls room, and sat on the bed, remembering the life I had when my mom was alive and how so soon everything was so drastically changed, I started to cry. I did not hear anyone come in the room, because I was taken up in my own thoughts until I heard "Tina are you alright" I quickly wipe the tears from my eyes and came face to face with Jack, one of my brothers friend. Embarrassed I told Jack "I was O.K" and immediately I left the room and went into the garden to pick the vegetables. I left the basket of vegetable on the front step and went into the kitchen to collect the dirty dishes. When I got back outside Jack had the basket of vegetables in his hand. I told him to give me the basket, because I was leaving, he said he would carry the basket for me, because he was going to accompany me halfway down the road. He took the basket and began walking down the road with me. I pleaded with Jack to turn back, but Jack just "kept on walking". I was afraid that someone would tell my aunt that I was walking down the road with a boy and I would get the biggest licking (spanking) of my life. I remembered the spanking I got when I was talking to my friend from another church, who was working with family planning. My aunt saw us talking and thought we were discussing birth control. After cursing me out and calling me demeaning names she gave me the finest licking.

This made me plead with Jack even more to go back. did not dare to tell Jack that I will get in trouble. If someone told my aunt that I was walking down the road with him, I will be in trouble.

I guess Jack heard the panic in my voice and then he said, "I will turn back under one condition".

I said what. Anything"

He said, "I want to see you tonight"? I promised to see Jack, but not intending to keep that promise.

Pastor Neverson laughed.

About eight o clock, that night my brother Winston, came in and said "Tina, Auntie Clair wants to see you", Auntie Clair was my grandmother's sister, who was living about half a block. Every night she would call me and share her dinner with me. I got up to go, when Winston said to me "wait I will accompany you" I waited for my brother and both of us walked out the door together.

When we got outside, he told me that it was not Auntie Clair, it was Jack. I told my brother that I did not want to see Jack, because he is too fresh".

Winston laughed and asked me why I said that?

I told him, "he said he love me". I was about to turn back to go inside the house, when Winston held on to my hand and said to me, "go and talk to him, it is ok for a boy to love you", he told me.

Winston followed me to where Jack was waiting and he said to Jack, "if ever you hurt my sister, you would have to deal with me". Jack told me how much he loved me that night, and that he loved me for a long time and never said anything. Then he asked me the saddest question "do you love me Tina?"

I answered" "I don't know".

He said to me, "do you know "what I don't know "means I said, "yes I don't know"

Pastor Neverson smiled.

Then Jack said, "I don't know means Yes and you are afraid or embarrassed to say yes", and by that Jack took me in his arms and kissed me. It was my first kiss, a long and hard kiss I felt every nerve in my body shivered, I pulled away from him and ran all the way home.

That night I could not sleep all I could hear jack's telling me how much he loved me and feeling his lips on mine. Many times, I would pinch myself to feel if it were real or if I were dreaming. I started seeing Jack every weekend, and I could not wait for Saturday to go up Decasa hill to get the vegetables, knowing Jack will be waiting up there for me. Jack and I started dating We dated for over a year, and by this time I grew to love Jack and were looking forward for the times when I could see him and be with him. I saw jack almost every day, because I was now taking sewing lessons in the Green Park valley with my aunt Nola. Jack was teaching in Green Park Valley School, and Auntie Nola was living a few blocks from the school. Jack waited for me every morning, and we would walk up the street together. On evenings, he will accompany me halfway home. I felt like Cinderella, the story my Kindergarten teacher told us, and Jack was my prince who came and swept me off my feet."

Pastor Neverson smiled.

"No good thing last forever, and I could not believe this will be the end of Jack and me. It was a Saturday night, about 7:30 Jack and Winston walked in our house, which he never did. He asked Auntie Tess if he can talk to me outside for a minute.

Auntie Tess turned to me and said "Tina, this young man would like to talk to you".

Embarrassingly, I got up and walked out the door

behind Jack. We went in the back yard and by the time I got outside I blurred out "what are you thinking?" and before I could say another word, Jack pulled me into his arms and kissed me. It was a long and hard kiss. Jack held me for a long time, as if he would never let me go, then he told me to sit down.

We sat on the back steps of the house then Jack pulled me into his arms, making me sit in his lap and his arms around me, he began talking to me. "It was a pleasure teaching you to grow up, but I cannot see you again", I steered at Jack with disbelief. Is this sick joke? I could not believe what I was hearing.

I jumped up out of his lap, "why? Why?" I kept asking him, "you don't love me anymore? What did I do"? I started crying.

Jack took me in his arms and dried my tears, he said, Tina "I want you to listen to me; I love you so much and I will always love you, but it is not possible for me to be with you right now", I asked him again, "why"? He said, "it has nothing to do with you, but I am leaving for Crown Island tomorrow".

"I knew Jack's parents were in Crown Island and they were arranging to get their children, but I never realized it was so soon. Pastor Neverson the funny thing about all this, Crown Island is where my father is."

I cried and begged Jack not to leave me; Jack was the best thing that ever happened to my whole rotten life.

When I was with Jack I forgot all the problems I was having at home, he made me feel like a person, he made me feel special and I was not even thinking of my father when I was with Jack. He took off his gold chain, that he was wearing and put it on around my neck, then he kissed me, it was a long and passionate kiss. He promised he will come back to me and that he would write to me every day and asked me to wait for him.

By this time, I heard Auntie Tess calling, telling me it was time for me to come inside, because she was going to bed. I got up to go inside when Jack took me in his arms again for the last time and kissed me. This was the last time I saw and heard about jack."

"What happened," Pastor Neverson asked with disbelief.

"I cried all night for weeks, especially on Saturdays. The days turned to weeks and the weeks became months, and I never got a letter from Jack, Pastor, he never wrote.

Pastor Neverson's face turn sad and said, "what happened Tina?'

"I do not know, but by then I started to believe that all men are the same, and Jack were just like my father But Pastor Neverson what's done in darkness must be revealed in the light".

Pastor Neverson said "so true Tina".

"One day Auntie Tess and I had a verbal fight and she blurred out "I know you have man, so go into the latrine for the letters your man from Crown Island is writing you"

"I was speechless, I could not believe what I was hearing. My aunt was getting my letters all this time and was reading them and then threw them in the latrine.

"What!" Pastor Neverson exclaimed.

"I could not help wondering what Jack thought of me, not knowing I never got his letters. I never forgot Jack. I always wondered what path my life would have taken with Jack and me."

Chapter 16

"After jack, I started looking for love in all the wrong places and choose men just like my father who didn't love me and who did not care, so I pledge to myself that I would wait on the man God has for me, and I pledged to be a virgin bride."

"One night we were hanging out in Ossie's van. Ossie used to date my sister Lou- Lou but when he came to our house to see my sister, all the girls would hang out in his van. then in the late part of the night, Ossie and Lou- Lou would leave. One night we were in Ossie's van, and then I saw him. A car pulled alongside the van and this boy came out. He was tall, dark and handsome. I could not take my eyes off him and at the same time! I did not want anyone to see me staring at him. He came out the car and into the van and talked to Ossie for a couple hours and then he left."

"I was head over heel in love with this man, a man I did not know and only saw him for a few hours, but I dare not ask Ossie who he was."

Pastor Neverson smiled and said, "that's interesting!"

"I would lay awake on my bed at night thinking about this boy. In the morning when I was all alone, I wrote this poem:

Love at first sight By Tina

I had one glance of him

I fell in love instantly

How can that be?

Am I insane, or am I going insane

I saw him for just for a moment?

My feelings were bought to light

As I gazed into his eyes from a distance

I felt the warm and joy of being in lo

I would lay awake on my bed at night

Thinking of him, would it be a dream in the morning

Or what would tomorrow bring.

Would he know how much I love him?

Or would my heart break again?

I have search deep down into my heart, looking for answers

And even to the utmost part of my soul

And found what was buried years ago; "Love"

A feeling I was afraid to accept

Afraid of being hurt again, afraid of the tears

But I cannot go on being afraid forever

I must face reality.

He has taken the other half of my apple

Now I am no longer the whole.

"Pastor, months passed, and I did not see this person again. I began to wander if he even existed. I did not speak to anyone about him, not my sisters, and not even Ossie. I kept this man a mystery and did not speak to anyone about him. In August of that year, our Church's youth group, to which I was president, planned a pelau party and a dance at the School for fundraising. We arranged for the event, and each member was placed at different stations. I told them I would float, because I did not want a be at a single station. I wanted to oversee everything to make sure everything was in order."

Pastor Neverson replied, "Good for you, that was being a real leader to take control."

Tina P.

"I was in the bar arranging the drinks and setting up the food, when I heard Ossie's voice speaking to me. I looked up and saw him, he was with Ossie and Linda 's boyfriend Jon, but pastor Neverson, what was ironic is the three men were wearing the same shirts, even the same color. I froze and at that time, then I pulled myself together and said in a calm voice What happening to you guys tonight wearing the same shirts Are you the band of brothers? Then I left the bar I went to the dance room and spoke to the band manager. By the time I got back in the bar this guy was outside speaking to a girl from my village. My heart sank as I walked into the bar. Ossie called to me and asked me what I was drinking. I accepted the drink from Ossie and started speaking to him. He walked into the bar and sat there for a little while, pretending that I did not notice him walking in. By the time he ordered a drink, I got up, left the bar, and went again to the dance hall. I dance by myself for a little while and when I saw him entered the door into the dance hall. I waited until he got in and again I was playing cat and mouse, I began to make my exit; I was heading for the door, when he grabbed my hand and then he spoke " 'Why are you running away from me all night". I was about to defend myself, by saying why do you think I am running from you? When the band start playing this tune; "When I see her, I am Gonna give her all the love I've got now" by the temptation. He pulled me into his arms, and we danced all night. He told me his name was Hud, and he was Ossie's half-brother living in the City. That was the start of a relationship for over fifteen years with Hud and I. Hud would come to the Green Park valley every weekend just to see me. I always looked forward to the time when I could be with Hud.

One night Hud came to see me, he was driving Ossie's van, Ossie was sitting in the passenger seat, when he dropped off Ossie, Hud did not get out of the van, I went and sat in the van with him. We talked for a while, then he asked me if I want to go for a ride. I was sitting with the van door open and my feet hanging out of the door. I did not answer him, but I put my feet inside the van and closed the door, put on the seat belt, then Hud drove off. We drove down to the college where he used to teach. Hud took me in his arms and started kissing me, long and passionate kisses and before I knew it, we ended up making love."

Chapter 17

Our youth group, had an Island youth camp, going to Lucian Island, one of the neighboring Islands. All the youth in our churches were invited. The next week I left for youth camp and I was gone for three weeks It was at camp that I realized I did not have my monthly cycle."

"I felt very anxious, and could not stop myself from worrying, wondering if I were pregnant. Could I get pregnant the first time I really had sex? I would withdraw myself from the crowd, go and sit underneath a tree in the school yard where we were camping. I was alone with my thought when I saw Nick car drove up; Nick was a Lucian whom I made friends with while I was at camp. He would come every evening and take four of the girls out site seeing, so by this time Nick and

I had become friends. Nick got out of the car and took one look at me and said, "wait in the car for me", then he left, he got in the car and was about to drive off, I said "what are you doing? I have to get permission from Smithy", who was our youth Pastor, before I can leave the campground, he said, "I already got permission" and he drove off. I asked him where we are going. "I am taking you to the mourn, you need to talk, you look like you just lost your best friend and needed a friend and I am going to be your listening ear and a shoulder for you to cry on".

We stop in this open green pasture with trees and flowers as far as eyes could see. with the beauty of the city below. We came out and sat on the grass, I cried and cried, and I told Nick everything of my completely rotten life.

Nick listened without a word. When we got up to leave, he said "you look like you need a hug; can I hug you"; I said "off course", it was the best friendship hug I ever experience. We drove back in silence.

On the way back to the camp, Nick stopped at a small building, which looked like a clinic, he said come, I would like you to meet a friend of mine. I said Nick, I am in no mood meeting anybody, look at my eyes, and they are all swollen from crying. Nick was very sarcastic; come on it is your eyes! I came out the car and walked in the building with Nick. A woman was in the other room, wearing a nurse uniform, Nick went in and talked to her. The woman came out and addresses me as Tina and said come with me. I trusted Nick, and one thing I learn for this past three weeks I had known him is not to argue with him.

I followed the woman and went with her, she told me Nick told her I am afraid that I might be pregnant, she hugs me and said let us make sure. She handed a small plastic cup and tell me she needed some urine. When I came out the toilet Nick was in the room with her, I handed her the cup and sat down, Nick came and sat beside me. He squeezes my hand and calmly said you are trembling, by this time the nurse came out and said, turning to Nick, she is pregnant. Nick put his hand around me as we walked to the car. When we got to the car, I brook down a and start crying again, I did not want to go back to the camp in this condition, and it was as if Nick read my mind. he took out his phone and made a call. Talking to the person on the on the other end, he apologized for not getting me back in time for dinner, but if its o.k. he will take me to eat, then he thank the person he was talking to. When he came off the phone, he said I was talking to your counselor. I told him I was taking you out to eat.

We went to a small deli and I poured out my heart to Nick, I told him my biggest fear was, if Hud would said the baby is not his, because it was only one time he had sex with me. This was when Nick educated me, how a person can become pregnant, even if is the only time that person had sex. I started to cry again; Nick hugged me as if he will not let me go; all I am saying "I want to go back home".

The first trip was leaving in two days to go back home, to Carib Island, so the next morning I went in Smithy's office and ask him, if I can leave on the first plain out and he said yes, the first trip is leaving on Wednesday. That Tuesday night Nick came to see me, let us go for a ride, I ask him where he was taking me and he said home, I said home where? And he said I live somewhere remember. We drove around for a while, and as we were driving into the driveway, I saw a lady came out and close the door, I felt uncomfortable, and asked Nick if his mom was expecting us, and he said yes, I blurred out "so why that woman came and lock the door", he said "are you mad with the woman to lock her own door. Anyway, this is not the only entrance", follow me. We entered the house through the back door. We had to walk through the kitchen into the dining room then into the living room. The house was in darkness as we entered the living room, his brother was on the piano, and he start playing "this is the time when we must say goodbye, then the light were turn on, and most of the youth from youth camp was there including Smithy. Nick took me in his arms, and we danced. then he whispered in my ear, "you understand now why my mom came and lock the door", I look him in the eyes, and smile. I left Lucian Island that Wednesday to go back to Carib Island; Nick met me at the airport to say his final goodbyes.

As soon as I landed at the airport, in Carib Island I called Hud and told him I was home and we had to talk. That night Hud was at a party at his aunt's house. About nine o clock that night a car pulled up at my gate and the driver was a person I knew very well, telling me Hud was at a party at Aunt Alice house and he send him for me. I told him I had a headache but tell Hud I will see him tomorrow. Pastor Neverson, getting pregnant at a young age and not married was a taboo and a shame and disgrace. I was everything in my church, youth leader, Sunday School teacher and some Sundays I was asked to preach. At youth camp I made the decision to go to seminary to become a youth pastor and now this! I was stripped of all my positions in church and was not allowed to go back to church, until the baby was born.

Smithy, our pastor at that time, will make home visit and would always come to my house to visit me, but he never had the chance to see me. Every time I saw his car, when he is coming to visit, I will run out the back door and go in the garden to hide, until he left."

"Pastor Neverson I had a rough pregnancy, the baby was always breech, so I had to be hospital two months before the delivery date. But thank God I had the support from Hud, he would come to the hospital every night to see me and stayed until the late hours in the night. My brother Irwin would also come to see me every night. I really used to look forward for their visits. Pastor Neverson, you will not guess who else came and visit me I really think God has a sense of humor.

Pastor Neverson replied, "Smithy, your pastor."

"How did you know"

Pastor Neverson laughed.

The first time I was so embarrassed, but after that,

he would come and visit me every week; I really used to look forward for his visit."

"Pastor Neverson, I always hear my grandmother say during life we are in death, this saying come to pass for me, but I was not ready for it."

Pastor Neverson said, "Tina I think we had enough for today, I will see you next week; I want you to continue to read psalm 139".

"I will Pastor, it is a nice psalm and I think that psalm is speaking to me, it now became my favorite psalm"; Pastor Neverson said "I am glad" and we were dismissed

Chapter 18

"Death is nothing to wonder about, today we are here and tomorrow we are gone. Pastor a next story I am about to tell you shattered my world. One Saturday evening Irwin came to visit, to be exact it was Easter Saturday, I noticed he was drinking. My brother was very intelligent, he was a teacher, but he had an alcohol problem, I talked to him about his drinking, He said, sis I don't want you to worry, just take care of yourself and the baby. That was the last conversation I had with my brother."

"That Easter Sunday I did not see Irwin, it was the only time my brother did not come to see me, I was a bit disappointed, but knowing my brother I figured he was late and didn't ask for permission to come and visit me. By this time two nurses came into the room to take my vitals, and on their way out. One nurse turns and look at me and said your brother is downstairs, the other nurse pulls her out of the room. Irwin never came up to see me."

I woke up Easter Monday which was a holiday With this guy who was running for election came to see me, I knew him, he went to school with my brothers and would hang out at De Casa with my brothers, We started talking politics for a while, then Auntie Eve, and Auntie Freda came in. Tommy told me he would be back. I said to my aunts, "what are you all doing here so early, I did not even realize it was a holiday. Auntie Freda said that she was by her sister, and she called Auntie Eve to come and pick her up to bring her to see me. At this time, a nurse came in and said let her eat first. The nurse brought my breakfast, then Tommy came in, "I am here to see you eat", he said jokingly. He kept joking with me while I was eating, and for the first time I ate all my breakfast. After I finish eating, we started talking about Winston and Irwin, this is when I got the news that my brother was killed on his way coming to the hospital, coming to see me."

Pastor Neverson sighed "Tina how did you take it", "Pastor Neverson, my whole world shattered. My brothers were the only father figures in my life, and now I am here ready to become a parent, the closest person to a father is gone" and I broke down and started to scream."

The doctors were waiting for this moment, now four doctors rushed into my room, all I am crying and said "I want to go home", My doctor said "Tina I cannot send you home if you are crying like this. It will not be good for you and the baby. You and the baby could die, and this will kill the rest of your family. You brother is dead, they cannot take on anymore",

I promise Dr. Lo I will not cry, and Auntie Eve, promise to take care of me, while I am home if she agreed to send me home. After the funeral, I went back to the hospital, my baby was born two weeks later."

All my other siblings were overseas. I was the only one who was left in Carib Island. Things started to get rough for me, the little salary I was working for as a post mistress could not make ends meet, so I asked my sister Lou-Lou to send an invitation letter for me to come to Paradise Island. I went to Bimsha to apply for a visa, and I got the Visa.

Chapter 19

"After I came to the Paraside Island, I had to prove I was not dumb, as my aunt thought, I applied to go to community college, The main request was a high school diploma and I did not have one, because I never went to high school. When I told the people at the admission desk my story, They called the superviser and explain my situation to him. Pastor Neverson, I was so scared, so I kept praying all the time. Then he turned to me and said to me "we are going to give you a chance if you pass the basic entrance level exam, and if you pass the Tesst, we will accept you into college.

On January second I started community college, got my Associate Degree and then went on to University for my Bachelors.

Pastor Neverson start clapping and said "good for you".

My phone rang, I looked at the number and said to Pastor Neverson, it is an overseas call maybe it is my Dad. Can I be excused for a minute; I would like to take this call. Pastor Neverson said sure. I got up and went into the chapel to answer the call. When I came back in the room where Pastor Neverson was, I was incredibly sad. Pastor Neverson took one look at me and knew something was wrong. "What happened Tina, are you all right"? Pastor Neverson asked. The call was from a hospital in Crown Island my dad had a stroke and a massive heart attack. He is asking for me. I started to cry. "Pastor Neverson" I cried, "I love my dad, although, he was never there for me, but I cannot go, I have no money". Pastor Neverson came over and patted me, and said "give me the information, and let me see what I can do". I give her the information of the caller and give her the phone. She talks to the person on the other end of the phone, then she said to me as soon as I work out something, I will call you. She dismissed with a prayer and I left.

Going to Crown Island to see a man who is supposed to be my father, who I hardly knew, it was not a trip

I was looking forward too, Pastor Neverson called me that evening, she told me she will pick me up in the morning to take me to the Airport. I said "O.K". and thank her. When I came off the phone with pastor Neverson, I started picking what little I had in a bag pack, and started to get ready for my trip,

The next days I boarded a plane to Crown Island, all expenses paid by the church for me to go and see my dad. I was all taken up in my own thoughts, when I heard the flight attendance voice over the intercom, "please fasten your seat belt and prepare for landing; we are now arriving at Queen B airport".

When I got off the plain, a man who was wearing a black pastoral robe who greeted me "Hi, Tina how was your flight? p Neverson told me all about you. I am Rev. Harry, I am sorry to hear about your father, I am sorry we could not meet in a much more pleasant situation". "Thank you Rev Harry it was so kind of you to pick me up and make arrangement for me to stay at the Methodist Mince, I appreciate it very much", Rev Harry said "the pleasure is all mine". He introduced me to the staff a young woman by the name of Easter who took me to my room. After we had lunch, Rev Harry and I drove to the hospital. He pulled up in front a big old brick building with a white sign outside the gate. I felt my heart dropped as we walked into the building. He walked up to the receptionist who was seated at the desk He said Hello to the woman wearing a pink uniform and a white nurse cap they chat for a while and then introduce me. He seems to know his way around the hospital. We walked to the elevator and then pressed the three buttons the elevator took us up three flights and then came to a stop. The door open and then we walk a small distance into the nurse's station. All the nurses were wearing white uniform and a small white nurse hat on their head, again, Rev Harry seems to know the staff. After introducing me, the nurse pointed to a room on the right side from the nurse's station.

"I'm really glad you had me, and I'm so sorry that we didn't know each other better". These were the words I was rehearsing in my head to say to my father.

Some things are impossible to plan. When someone thinks of the last words that you say to someone dying, the moment is so profound yet surreal, that you feel like you are in a walking dream. I tried to gather myself, and breathe, but there is no way of knowing how to act or react, so I just go.

Walking down the hospital hallways, I tried my best

to remember everything, the smells, and the shapes of the numbers on the doorways, faces of passing people, wondering about their moments here and how it would affect them for the rest of their lives.

I tried my hardest to be present, to focus on everything, while looking for the little details hundreds of pictures taken with my eyes, because although I might forget the overall feeling of today, those little things I learned remains with me.

She saw me looking around like an aimless child, and without thinking, grabbed my hand, looked at me and smiled. We are here she said, just walk straight its 11A.

As a child, I had this dream that I was walking with my mom down the corridors of the airport, both holding hands, bursting with joy, for the arrival of the plane that carried my dad. That day in my dream, it was so sunny, that yellow radiated through the windows and completely covered everything as if we were walking through a field of sunflowers. The warmth that comes over me just remembering this dream, similar now to this hugged given by my father's common law wife. A person I once hated, who destroyed my family, now was my surrogate mother in this moment.

Chapter 20

I held my breath, pushed the door and open my eyes, the scene, similar to most we've seen in movies, or bad soap opera, a person lying still, machines everywhere, beeping of a heart monitor, bland colors, chill in the air.

I had built this moment up so many times in my mind, then being frustrated, and excited at the same time. With an impulse, I rushed over to the bed held my face as close as possible to his, and just starred, counting the moles, freckles, peaks and valleys of wrinkles on his face.

There he is, I said to myself, this lifeless man is my father who I was in search of my whole life

I expected to feel anger because I was a truly angry person. Anger is a very seductive emotion, the truth is that holding on to anger is an act of a coward, bitterness eats you from inside out, and it blinded your eyes from the many opportunities that would help you heal and grow. The cure to bitterness is learning to forgive and learning to accept that all unkindness, unloving and unjust act is a result of the pain I was feeling all these years I expected to feel sadness, but instead I just felt nothing. I just smiled. So much to say, so many questions, what is the point? Was it even going to be heard, is this for him or for me?

I leaned over

"Hey, it is me, Tina: five of six.

My daughter, your granddaughter has moles just like you.

My favorite color is blue, I tell people black, but that is a lie. To some people black is ugly, as they put it "black is the color of dirt", blackness was what I saw all these years

Irwin were my favorite of all my siblings, because in my head, his personality is what I would hope you would be like. Quiet, confident, and sensitive to the ones he loved, but notoriously bad.

My favorite moment as a child was playing outside in the rain, while the sun shines brightly at the same time. The rainwater felt as warm as a bath, and I always imagined God was playing with us as well by making that happen.

All the years I've lived on this earth, I'm not sure I've really learned anything, and I'm still figuring things out every day, that's my favorite thing about life. I still cannot ride a bike, and never learned to swim, and I am not sure if I have found the love of my life yet, maybe I never will.

Either way

I love you.

I am glad you had me, and I am so sorry that we did not know each other better.

Thanks dad".

This was the last conversation I had with my father, after he had abandoned his wife and six children.

There are so many things I kept hidden, but until I heal my past wounds and come to peace with it, the past would continue to haunt me, those painful experiences would continue to have power over me, and I would continue to be their victim.

As I walked down the hall way from my father's room, I saw a room with the sign mark Chapel I walked in, as I knelt at the alter to pray, allowing the tears to flow down my cheeks I felt the wonderful calmness of an inner quietness, an inner peace. This was when I felt someone arms around me as I rose from the alter, I found what I was searching for, in the end what I wanted all these years.

A search for my parent brought me to my father death bed to witness my father breathe his last breath, holding this woman hand, I whispered these words "Rest in peace daddy".

Rev Harry dropped me back at the Airport. Waiting to board the plane back to Paradise Island ; I ponder, "In search of my parent for all these years did not give me the answer I was looking for, but it give me inner peace and forgiveness" . As the songwriter puts it "The answer my friends must come from within; the answer must come from within".

Printed in the United States
By Bookmasters